MW00892853

Animal Friends

point and say

Animal Friends
a first word and picture book

HERMES
HOUSE

First published in 1998 by Hermes House
27 West 20th Street, New York, NY 10011

HERMES HOUSE books are available for bulk purchase for sales promotion and for premium use.
For details, write or call the sales director, Hermes House, Anness Publishing Inc.,
27 West 20th Street, New York, NY 10011; (800) 354-9657

© Anness Publishing Limited 1998

Hermes House is an imprint of
Anness Publishing Limited

All rights reserved. No part of this publication may be reproduced, stored in a retrieval system, or transmitted in any way or
by any means, electronic, mechanical, photocopying, recording or otherwise, without the prior written permission of the
copyright holder.

ISBN 1–84038–154–X

Publisher: Joanna Lorenz
Designer: Julie Francis

Picture Credits:
Bruce Coleman, Ecoscene, Holt Studios, FLPA, Nature Photographers, Papillio Photographic,
Planet Earth Pictures, Tony Stone, Warren Photographic/Jane Burton, Zefa Pictures

Printed and bound in Hong Kong/China

1 3 5 7 9 10 8 6 4 2

Contents

Farm Animals

Wild Animals

Pets

Farm

Animals

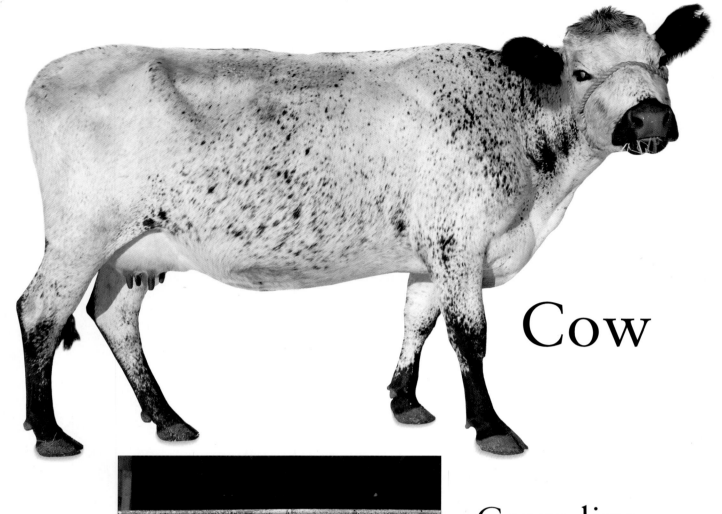

Cow

Cows live
in a
cowshed.

Cows live
together in
big groups
called herds.

Calf

A baby cow is called a calf.

Calves drink their mother's milk.

Cows look after their calves in the cowshed.

Horse

Many horses live on farms.

Horses eat grass.

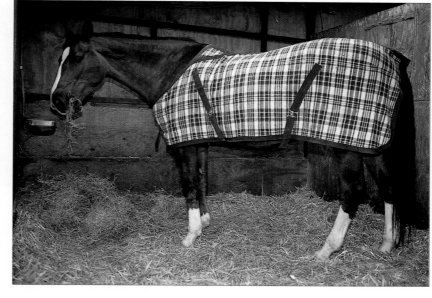

Some horses sleep in a warm stable at night.

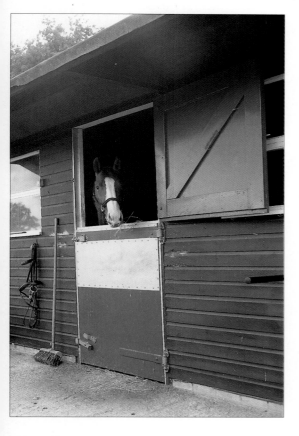

A horse can see over the stable door.

Inside the stable there is food and water for the horse.

hay

pony nuts

water

Foal

A baby horse is
called a foal.

Foals can
stand up
as soon as
they are
born.

Foals eat grass with their mothers.

Foals live in the stable too.

Look at my long, thin legs!

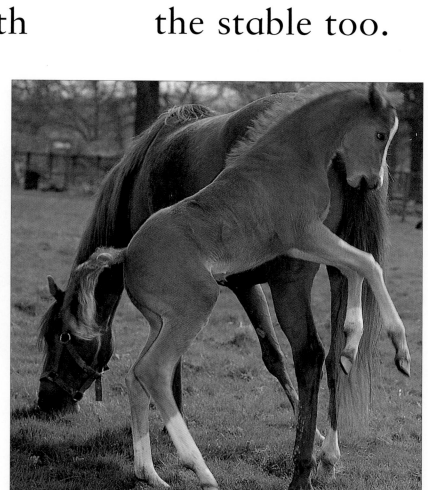

Foals like to play.

Pig

Pigs root around in the ground to find things to eat.

Mother pigs have little pink piglets.

Piglet

A baby pig is called a piglet.

Piglets have curly tails.

Piglets live in a sty.

Piglets have lots of brothers and sisters.

Sheep

Sheep have long, woolly coats. Sheep like to eat hay.

Sheep live in big groups called flocks.

A baby sheep is called a lamb. Little lambs nuzzle close to their mothers to keep warm and safe.

Sheep live in fields.

Goat

Goats
have long
beards.

They live
in fields.

Kid

A baby goat is called a kid.

Kids stay close to their mother.

Duck

Ducks dive into the water to find their food.

Ducks like to live near water.

Ducks can walk...

and fly...

and swim.

Duckling

Baby ducks
are called
ducklings.

Ducklings
like to play
with their
mothers.

Ducklings
live in a nest.

Soon it is
time for their
first swim.

Ducks have
special feet
for swimming.

Chicken

Chickens live on farms.

Chickens peck and scratch the ground to find corn and seeds to eat.

Chickens eat corn.

Chickens eat and sleep in a chicken coop.

The coop has a door and a ramp.

Chickens lay eggs.

Chick

A baby chicken is called a chick.

Chicks hatch out of eggs.

Chicks
are fluffy.

They soon
grow feathers.

Dog

A dog
helps the
shepherd
bring the
sheep
home.

Baby dogs are
called puppies.
They learn
how to help
on the farm.

Most dogs are
kept as pets.

Do you know a
friendly dog?

Cat

Cats keep
all the
mice away
from the
farm.

Baby cats are called kittens. They like to chase mice too...

they also like to have a nap.

Bees

Honeybees
collect pollen
from flowers.

These bees are kept
in wooden boxes
called hives.

Thousands
of bees
live in the
hive.

The beekeeper wears special clothes.

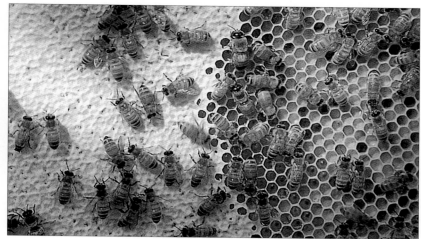

Bees make honey inside the hive.

honeycomb

Honey is good to eat.

Can you match the right name

dog

sheep

cat

chicken

goat

horse

pig

duck

to the right animal?

Wild
Animals

Lion

Lions are big and furry and live in hot countries.

They have a
very loud roar
and sharp,
pointed teeth.

Chimpanzee

Chimpanzees like to swing from trees.

Chimpanzees carry their babies around with them. The baby has to hold on very tightly.

Tiger

Tigers are big and fierce. They have striped fur.

Tigers have long whiskers and big paws.

Baby tigers are called cubs.

Cubs are
fierce too.

Giraffes live in
hot countries.

Giraffe

A giraffe's long neck helps it to
reach the tops of tall trees but...

bending
down is not
so easy!

Crocodile

Crocodiles have big
teeth and scaly bodies.

Crocodiles are fierce hunters. They can even stand up in rivers to catch birds to eat.

Zebra

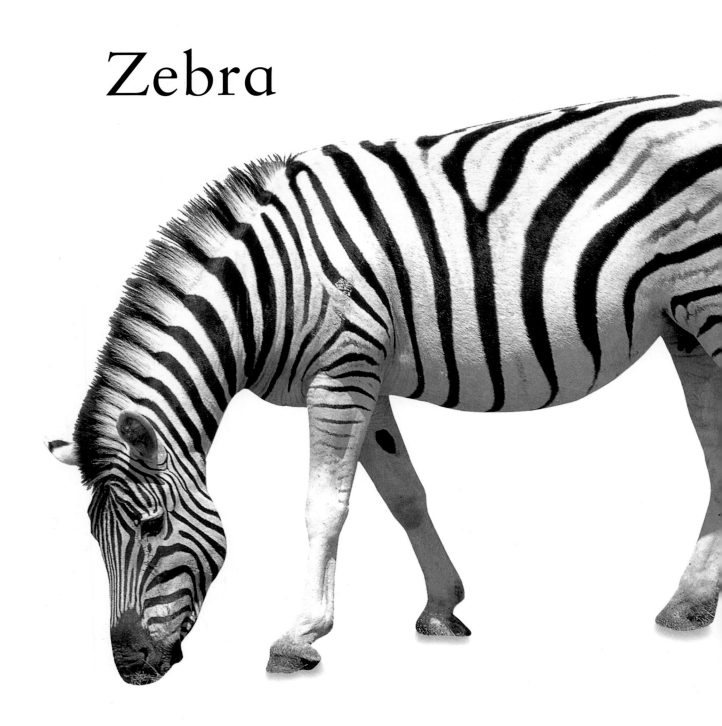

Zebras are striped.

Baby zebras are called foals. They drink their mother's milk.

Zebras live together in big groups called herds.

Polar bear

Polar bears
live in very
cold places.

Polar bears love to play in snow and ice.

Polar bears have thick, soft fur to keep them warm. Baby polar bears are called cubs.

Elephant

Elephants have long trunks and large ears.

They are very big with wrinkled skin.

They use their trunks to
suck up water...

and then
squirt it
into their
mouths.

Kangaroo

Kangaroos
live in
Australia.

They jump high
into the air on
their strong
back legs.

Mother kangaroos keep their babies
safe in a special pocket called a pouch.

Penguin

Penguins have long beaks to catch fish to eat.

Penguins live in cold places.

Penguin families cuddle
up together to keep warm
in the snow and ice.

Snake

Snakes are long
and scaly.

Snakes slither along
the ground on their
bellies.

They like to coil around the branches of trees.

They do not have arms or legs.

Frog

Frogs have
bulging eyes
and slimy skin.

They live
in ponds
and rivers.

Frogs like waterlilies and jump from leaf to leaf.

Baby frogs are called tadpoles. They change into frogs when they grow up.

Are there any frogs near you?

Bird

Many birds live in gardens. They like to eat nuts.

Tiny birds build nests in wooden nesting boxes.

You can leave food for them on bird-feeding tables.

Birds live in trees.

Birds make nests to live in, where they lay their eggs.

Can you match the right name

kangaroo

zebra

giraffe

crocodile

chimpanzee

Pets

Dog

Dogs have cold, wet noses and tails that wag when they are happy.

Dogs live in kennels, inside...

or outside.

Some dogs sleep indoors in a special basket.

Dogs need to be taken out for walks.

Puppy

Baby dogs are called puppies.

Puppies have lots of brothers and sisters.

Puppies drink their mother's milk.

They need lots of food to grow into big dogs.

They like to snooze.

Puppies like to play with toys.

They are very playful.

Puppies like to chase balls.

They like to
chew bones.

Puppies
like to be
stroked.

Rabbit

Pet rabbits live in a hutch.

Rabbits sip water from a bottle.

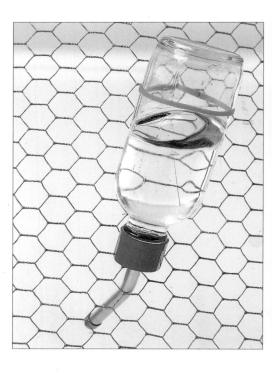

The hutch has a bedroom for the rabbit.

Rabbits have twitchy noses and long ears.

Hutches have straw on the floor.

Baby Rabbit

Baby rabbits hop
along the ground.

They live in a soft,
warm nest with
their mother.

They like to nibble on crunchy carrots...

and lettuce.

Carrots

Lettuce

Have you ever stroked a baby rabbit?

Fish

Fish can be pets. They live in a bowl...

or a tank.

They like to swim in clean water with rocks and plants.

They look for their food in the gravel.

Fish eat special food.

Gravel

Cat

Cats have soft fur, sharp claws and tickly whiskers.

Cats can have lots of kittens.

They like to watch fish.

Cats like to live with people. Have you ever stroked a cat?

Kitten

A baby cat is called a kitten.

Kittens have lots of brothers and sisters.

They sleep in baskets.

Kittens often wash
their fur...

and scratch.

They like to cuddle
up together.

Kittens
play with
toys...

and string.

Kittens like to climb.

They like to chase balls.

Have you ever played with a kitten?

Hamster

Hamsters are small and furry.

They live in cages.

They like to run around their cage.

Sawdust makes a warm bed.

Hamsters eat special food with nuts and seeds.

Hamsters run up ladders...

and hide in houses.

Horse

A horse is so strong it can carry a person on its back.

Horses like to gallop very fast.

You need to wear a helmet on a horse.

Horses wear a saddle and reins.

Horses live in stables.

Foal

Foals
are baby
horses.

They soon
grow into
strong horses.

They nibble grass...

and drink
lots of their
mother's
milk.

Tortoise

Tortoises sleep all
winter and wake up
in the summertime.

Tortoises have a hard shell.

They have
short legs.

Can you match the right name

hamster

cat

dog

tortoise

fish

horse

rabbit

to the right animal?